SOUL CHILD

A Reflective Healing Workbook

By Danita Ealy, MS, BCBA, LBA

For permission requests, contact the author.
ISBN: 979-8-9932278-1-8
Printed in the United States of America

Disclaimer: This workbook is intended for personal growth and reflection. It is not a substitute for professional therapy, diagnosis, or treatment. If you are experiencing significant distress, please seek the support of a licensed mental health professional.

For the child within us all, "still waiting" to be seen, heard, and loved.
May this book be a safe place for reflection, healing, and growth.

I dedicate this workbook to the little girl I once was and to every soul who has ever felt unseen or unheard. May you find in these pages the gentleness, understanding, and joy you have always deserved.

This workbook incorporates music as part of the healing journey because "Soul Child" reflects both the music that shapes us and the child within us. For many of us, music is tied to core memories, moments when a song captured exactly what we were feeling, or when hearing it for the first time marked a turning point in our lives. I know, personally, I can trace chapters of my own story back to the songs that carried me. Even if you don't consider yourself a music fan, I hope that the reflections here help you connect with your inner child, and that music becomes a companion to both the joy and the pain of life. It's not about erasing your past, but about holding it gently and transforming it into strength.
— Danita Ealy, MS, LPA, BCBA, LBA

WHY "SOUL CHILD" INSTEAD OF "INNER CHILD"?

You may be familiar with the term inner child, the younger part of us that carries memories, emotions, and beliefs from our earliest years. Those parts hold both joy and pain, wonder and wounds. In this workbook, I use the term "Soul Child" to describe that same tender part of ourselves, with a deeper emphasis. The word soul points to something lasting and essential — not only psychological, but also emotional and spiritual.

Your Soul Child is the essence of who you were before the world told you who to be, the part that longs for safety, love, and freedom, and the keeper of both your earliest wounds and your purest joys. Meeting your "soul" child is not just about looking back — it's about reconnecting with the deepest part of yourself that has always been waiting to be noticed and healed.

As a lifelong music lover, I often connect with my Soul Child through songs. Music has a way of giving voice to feelings we can't always name, reminding us that growth can emerge even in hard places, and that hope has always been within reach.

Music is Medicine. Music has the power to reach the parts of us that words alone cannot. A single melody can awaken long-forgotten memories, stir emotions we've tucked away, and soothe the deepest parts of our being. In our healing journey, music becomes more than sound—it becomes medicine for the heart, offering comfort, release, and reconnection to our Soul Child.

WHY MUSIC IS EFFECTIVE FOR TRAUMA & SOUL CHILD WORK

Music is beneficial in trauma healing because it bypasses the verbal-rational parts of the brain and connects directly to the limbic system, the brain's emotional center.

1. Emotional Expression and Access

Trauma survivors, including the inner child, often find it difficult to express intense or complex feelings with words.
- Non-Verbal Outlet: Music provides a safe way to express emotions like grief, anger, or fear without having to articulate them verbally, which can feel overwhelming.
- Accessing Memories: Certain songs or melodies can safely evoke memories and emotions associated with childhood experiences, allowing them to be processed.

2. Emotional and Physiological Regulation

Trauma causes dysregulation (heightened stress or emotional numbness). Music can help bring the body back into a more balanced state.
- Calming the Nervous System: Slow, soothing music can help to reduce anxiety, lower blood pressure, and decrease heart rate, promoting a state of relaxation and safety.
- Regulating Mood: Music can be used to manage emotional states, serving as a tool for self-soothing when a person feels triggered or overwhelmed.

3. Fostering Connection and Self-Compassion

Soul child work centers on re-parenting the wounded younger self with care and compassion.
- Connecting with the Soul Child: Using music can help create a safe, playful, or nurturing atmosphere, which aids in connecting with the vulnerable inner child part.
- Creative Expression: Like art therapy, music allows for a creative outlet (listening, lyrical analysis, or even creating your own music/playlist) that gives the inner child a voice and fosters a sense of empowerment.

IMPORTANT CONSIDERATION: WHEN TO SEEK PROFESSIONAL HELP

While a trauma workbook with music reflections can be a powerful self-help tool, it is important to remember that it is not a substitute for professional therapy.

If you have a history of significant or complex trauma, working through deep wounds can be highly activating and overwhelming. It's best to use this type of resource in conjunction with or under the guidance of a qualified mental health professional. They can provide the necessary support and grounding techniques to ensure the healing process is safe and regulated.

MEETING YOUR SOUL CHILD

Why Start Here?

Before healing can begin, we must first understand who we are healing. Deep inside each of us lives a younger version of ourselves — a tender soul who once laughed freely, dreamed boldly, and trusted fully. For some, that child feels vibrant and curious, still tugging at us to play, explore, and create. For others, that child feels hidden, carrying fear, sadness, or unmet needs, silenced by experiences that felt too big to carry at the time.

This "soul child" is not imaginary; it is the collection of memories, emotions, and core beliefs formed in our earliest years. These younger versions of ourselves still live within us, shaping how we see the world, how we relate to others, and even how we care for ourselves today. Sometimes, without realizing it, we continue to protect that child by avoiding certain feelings, people, or places. At other times, we may repeat old patterns because that younger part of us is still longing for comfort, love, or safety

In this first chapter, you are invited to gently meet your soul child — not with judgment, but with curiosity and compassion.
You will begin to:
- Notice the moments when your soul child speaks up in your reactions, your longings, or your vulnerabilities.
- Reflect on the stories, memories, or images that come to mind when you think of your younger self.
- Listen for what that child within you may be trying to tell you: their fears, their joys, their unspoken needs.
-

This process is not about reliving pain but about acknowledging presence. Your soul child may be scared, silenced, or simply waiting to be noticed. By slowing down, listening, and honoring that younger version of yourself, you create the foundation for true healing.

As you move through these pages, remember: you are both the child who needs care and the adult capable of providing it. Meeting your soul child is the first step toward wholeness, a chance to embrace all parts of yourself with love, understanding, and grace

Reflection: Who Is Your Soul Child?

When you think of yourself as a child, what age comes to mind first?

- *What is the earliest memory where you felt truly safe?*

- *What is a memory where you felt small, unseen, or misunderstood?*

Take a few minutes to jot down the images or feelings that surface. Don't judge them — simply notice.

_____

_____

_____

_____

_____

_____

_____

_____

Exercise: Drawing or Visualizing Your Soul Child

1. *Close your eyes. Picture yourself as a child. What are they wearing? What expression is on their face?*

2. *On the page below (or in your journal), sketch or describe what you see. If drawing feels hard, you might use a childhood photo for reference, or simply write what you remember: "wearing a blue t-shirt and jeans, holding a stuffed bear, looking shy*

3. *When you're ready, take a breath and gently acknowledge this younger version of yourself. You might say something simple like: "I see you. I remember you. You matter."*

Worksheet: Letter to My Younger Self

Complete the sentences below. Don't overthink — write what flows.

Dear little me, I remember when...

_____

_____

_____

_____

I know you felt...

_____

_____

_____

_____

What I wish someone had told you then is...

_____

_____

_____

_____

If I could be there for you, I would...

_____

_____

_____

_____

Today, I want you to know...

_____

_____

_____

Music Reflection Prompt

Think of a song from your childhood that still holds meaning. Play it and listen carefully.

- *What memories or emotions does it stir?*
- *How does your younger self respond to hearing it now?*
- *In what ways can music be a safe bridge between past and present?*

Write your reflections below.

_____

_____

_____

_____

_____

_____

_____

_____

_____

_____

_____

Closing Reflection: Meeting Your Soul Child

As you complete this first chapter, pause to honor the simple yet powerful step you've taken: noticing the presence of your soul child. You may have met them as a playful spirit, a shy voice, or a tender memory. However they appeared, they are a part of you, deserving of compassion, patience, and care.

Remember, you are not trying to "fix" this younger self. You are learning to see them, to listen, and to let them know they are no longer alone. Every time you pause to acknowledge your soul child, you strengthen the bridge between who you were and who you are becoming.

Take a deep breath and remind yourself: Healing begins with recognition. I have started the journey.

Closing Takeaway

Use the prompts below to gather your first impressions and insights from this chapter.
Prompts:
- *The most important thing I realized about my soul child is…*
- *One quality from my younger self I want to reconnect with is…*
- *One way I can begin caring for my soul child right now is…*

Use the space below to write your reflections.

_____

_____

_____

_____

_____

_____

Affirmation: "I see my Soul Child, and I hold space for their healing with love."

UNDERSTANDING YOUR WOUNDS

Before we can offer healing to our soul child, we must first pause to understand where the wounds began. None of us arrive in adulthood untouched by our past. The stories of our earliest years, both nurturing and painful, shaped how we learned to see ourselves, others, and the world around us. Some of these experiences may have left us with memories of warmth, safety, and belonging. Others may have left scars: times we felt unseen, unheard, or unworthy.

These wounds can take many forms. For some, they come from obvious experiences of loss, neglect, or trauma. For others, they may be more subtle, a lack of emotional support, unspoken expectations, or feeling pressured to be someone we were not ready to be. Regardless of their form, these moments leave imprints on our hearts and nervous systems. Over time, the child within us learns strategies to cope: hiding emotions, trying to be perfect, withdrawing, or becoming overly responsible. While these strategies once helped us survive, they may now prevent us from fully thriving.

This chapter invites you to gently uncover the sources of those hurts while staying safe and grounded in the present. You are not being asked to relive every painful memory. Instead, you are being guided to notice patterns, connect the dots, and recognize the messages your younger self received, messages that may still echo in your adult life.

To support you in this process, the exercises in this section will help you look at your story from different angles:

- Reflection: Early Messages You Received: You'll reflect on the words, lessons, and unspoken rules that shaped how you saw yourself and your place in the world.
- Exercise: Naming the Wounds: You'll give language to the hurts that still linger, allowing you to begin acknowledging them without shame or denial.
- Worksheet: Early Wounds Inventory: You'll organize and list out the specific wounds or patterns from childhood, identifying how they might still affect your thoughts, emotions, and relationships today.
- Music Reflection Prompt: You'll connect with songs that stir childhood memories — noticing how music can bring hidden emotions to the surface and give voice to what your soul child has carried.

By shining a light on these wounds, you begin to understand why your soul child reacts the way they do, why certain triggers feel so powerful, and why some parts of your life may feel harder to heal. Remember: becoming aware of your wounds is not about blame. It is about compassion and giving yourself permission to acknowledge what was difficult and offering your soul child the validation they may never have received.

As you move through the reflections, exercises, and worksheets in this chapter, take your time. Pause when needed. Stay grounded by noticing your breath, feeling your feet on the floor, or playing music that soothes you. You are safe now. You are no longer powerless. The child within you has been waiting not only to be noticed, but also to be understood. This chapter is your opportunity to listen, to name the hurts, and to begin loosening the hold they have on your story.

Reflection: Who Is Your Soul Child?

Think back to the atmosphere of your childhood home. What were some of the spoken or unspoken rules that guided daily life? Were there things you were encouraged to express, and other things you were expected to hide?

Consider how love was experienced in your family. Did you feel accepted and valued just as you were, or did it sometimes feel like love had to be earned through achievement, good behavior, or meeting certain expectations?

Reflect also on how the adults around you handled difficult emotions such as conflict, anger, or sadness. Were these feelings welcomed, ignored, or even punished?

Take your time as you explore these memories. Notice any themes or patterns that stand out. These early experiences may have become powerful messages that shaped how your Soul child learned to navigate the world and how you continue to relate to yourself and others today.

Exercise: Naming the Wounds

1. In the area below or on a piece of paper, write down the first few painful memories that come to mind when you think of your childhood.
2. Next to each memory, name the emotion that accompanies it (fear, shame, loneliness, sadness, anger, etc.).
3. Circle the one or two that feel most present in your life today.
4. Say to yourself: "It's okay to acknowledge this. I am safe now."

Memory	Emotion

Worksheet: Early Wounds Inventory

Use the prompts below to begin your inventory:

- *A time I felt unheard was…*
- *A time I felt unsafe was…*
- *A time I felt unloved was…*
- *A time I felt powerless was…*

As you write, remember this is not about blame. It's about giving your Soul child's pain a voice.

_____

_____

_____

_____

_____

_____

_____

_____

Music Reflection Prompt

Choose a song that reminds you of a difficult season in your childhood. Play it softly. Notice how your body reacts as the song plays. Do you tense up, feel heavy, or grow sad? Imagine sitting with your younger self as they listen to it. What would you want to say to them as the song plays?

Closing Reflection

You have taken brave steps by exploring the tender places your Soul Child still carries. Naming wounds is never easy, yet by acknowledging them you have already begun the process of healing. Remember, this work is not about blame, but about recognition. By giving voice to what once felt silenced, you honor the child within you and remind them they are no longer alone.

Think of one wound from your past that still echoes in your life today. Write a short letter to your Soul Child about this wound. You might:
- *Acknowledge what happened.*
- *Name the feelings connected to it.*
- *Offer words of comfort, reassurance, or safety that you wish they had heard then.*
Use the space below to write freely.

Closing Takeaway

- One wound I am ready to acknowledge is…
- Something I realized about how my past still affects me is…
- A way I can begin to care for my Soul Child moving forward is…

Affirmation: "I honor my Soul Child by acknowledging their pain. I am safe now, and I am moving toward healing with compassion and strength."

RECONNECTING WITH JOY AND PLAY

Healing your Soul Child is not only about understanding wounds. It is also about rediscovering the joy, curiosity, and playfulness that were once so natural. Joy and play are not luxuries; they are vital parts of healing. They remind us that laughter, imagination, and creativity are just as powerful as reflection and tears.

In this chapter, you will be invited to explore what once made you feel alive and free. Think back to the activities you loved as a child. Was it drawing, singing, dancing, playing outdoors, or simply daydreaming? Even if those moments felt brief or far away, they are still within you. By reconnecting with these experiences, you awaken parts of your Soul Child that long to feel safe, expressive, and seen.

These exercises are designed to help you bring joy back into your present life. They are not about "acting childish," but about reclaiming the playfulness and wonder that belong to you at every age.

How to Use the Exercises in This Chapter

Reflection: What Brought You Joy?
Remember the games, people, or moments that once made you feel safe and carefree, and notice whether they still show up in your life today.

Exercise: Rediscovering Play
 List activities you loved as a child, choose one to revisit, and give yourself time to enjoy it simply for fun. Afterwards, reflect on how it felt.

Worksheet: My Joy Map
Connect past joys to present ones, imagine new activities to try, and describe in your own words what joy feels like for you.

Music Reflection Prompt
Play an uplifting childhood song. Let yourself move or sing if you wish, then write about the feelings and memories it awakens in your Soul Child.

Reflection: What Brought You Joy?

Take a moment to reflect...
- What games, toys, or activities made you happiest as a child?
- What moments made you laugh the most?
- What experiences helped you feel carefree and lighthearted?

As you write, notice that you are reflecting on what brought you joy, not who. Focus on the simple things — the activities or moments that didn't require money, special training, or outside approval. Think of the joys that were natural, effortless, and free: splashing in the rain, humming a tune, making up stories, or discovering a talent you didn't know you had.

Joy in its purest form is not tied to possessions or performance. It is found in the simplest expressions of being alive. Take a few minutes to reflect on whether these joys still show up in your life today. If not, consider how you might invite that simple joy back into your world now.

What games, toys, or activities made you happiest as a child?

_____

_____

_____

What moments made you laugh the most?

_____

_____

_____

What experiences helped you feel carefree and lighthearted?

_____

_____

_____

My Simple Joys Today:

_____

_____

_____

Exercise: Rediscovering Play

- Write a list of activities you loved as a child (drawing, riding a bike, playing with dolls, reading comic books, dancing, etc.).
- Circle at least one of those activities that you could bring into your life this week in some form.
- Set aside 15–30 minutes this week to actually do that activity, not for productivity, but for pure enjoyment.
- Afterward, jot down how it made you feel.

- *Activities I enjoyed as a child:*

_____

_____

_____

- *Pick an activity that you plan to do in the next 7 days:*

_____

_____

_____

- *Schedule a day/time to do the activity:*

_____

_____

_____

- *Reflect on how you felt while completing the activity*

_____

_____

_____

My Joy Map

The Joy Map is a tool to help you see the connections between your past joys, your present joys, and the ways you can invite joy into your life today. It isn't about perfection or productivity — it's about remembering that joy is part of your healing journey. By mapping it out visually, you create a personal guide you can return to whenever you feel disconnected from play, laughter, or ease.

Use the prompts below to guide your Joy Map:
- As *a child, I loved…*
- *Today, I still enjoy…*
- A *new activity I'd like to try is…*
- *One small way I can invite more laughter into my life is…*
- *Joy feels like… (describe in your own words).*

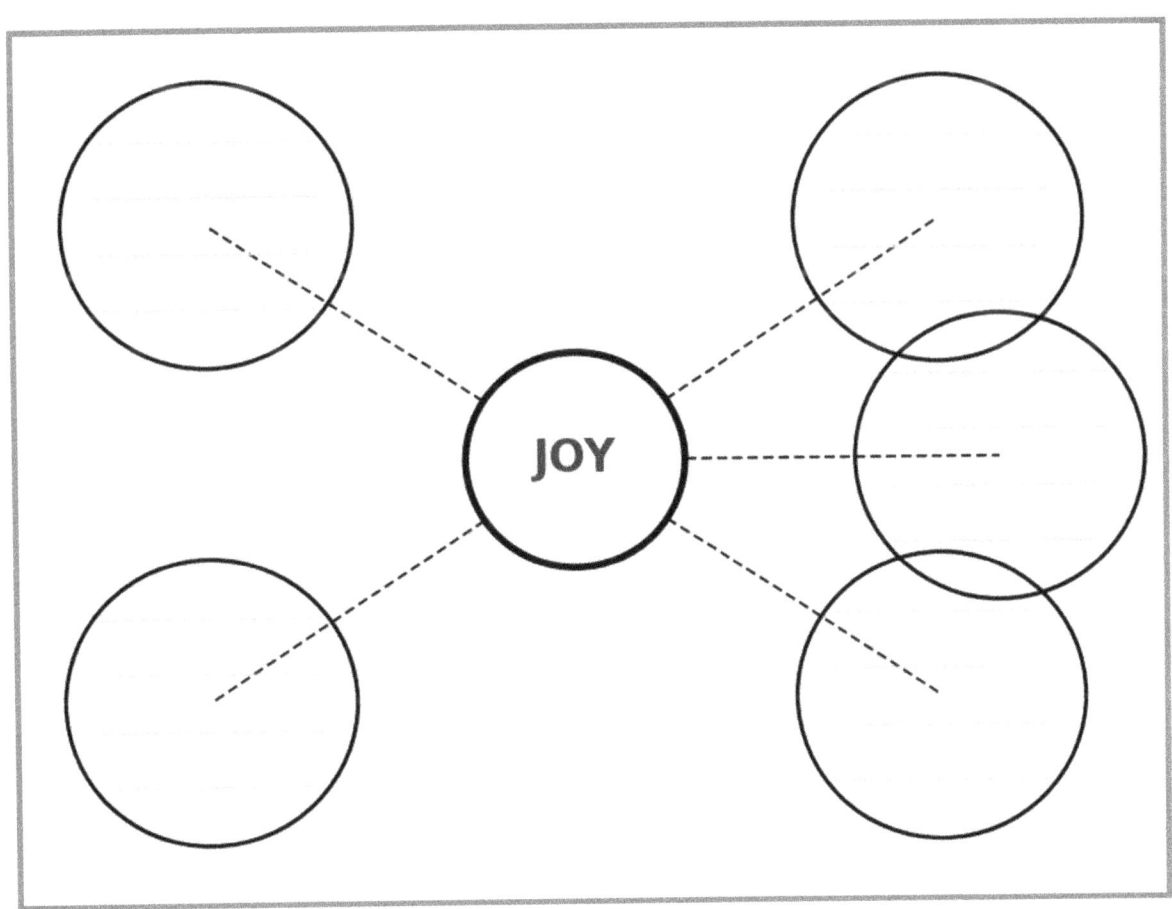

Music Reflection Prompt

Choose a fun or uplifting song from your childhood that made you want to dance or sing along. Play it now. Let yourself move, hum, or sway if it feels right. After listening, write about the sensations or memories it awakens in you, and how your Soul child responds to it.

Closing Reflection

Joy is not something you outgrow. It is something that waits for you to return. By remembering what once brought you delight, you have given your Soul Child permission to laugh, play, and create again. Even if those moments feel small, they remind you that healing is not only about tending wounds but also about reclaiming lightness, wonder, and fun.

Closing Takeaway

Take a few moments to capture what you want to carry forward from this chapter:
- *A joyful memory I want to hold onto is…*
- *One way I can invite play into my life this week is…*
- *Joy, for me, feels like…*

Use the space below to reflect in your own words.

_____

_____

_____

_____

_____

_____

_____

_____

Affirmation: "I welcome joy and play back into my life. My Soul Child is free to laugh, explore, and feel alive."

CREATING SAFETY AND SELF-COMPASSION

For your Soul Child to heal, they must first feel safe. Safety is the ground from which trust, healing, and compassion grow. Yet many of us did not grow up in environments where safety and kindness were consistent. Some of us felt physically vulnerable, others emotionally unprotected Those early experiences can still shape how we care for ourselves today.

In this chapter, you will explore what safety means to you and how to provide it for your Soul Child now. You'll reflect on the ways you once understood safety, how that definition has evolved, and what your Soul Child still longs for. You'll also begin creating practices that help you feel secure and supported in the present.

One way you'll do this is by imagining and even drawing a safe space for your Soul Child. This is not about artistic skill or creating a perfect picture. It's about giving shape and color to a feeling using imagery, symbols, or even doodles to express what safety looks and feels like for you. By making it visible, you create an anchor you can return to whenever you need comfort or grounding.

Through reflections, exercises, and music prompts, this chapter will help you practice offering your Soul Child the two things they need most: safety and compassion.

Reflection: What Safety Means to You

Take a moment to reflect on the following:
- *What did safety look like for you as a child?*
- *Did you feel safe physically? Emotionally?*
- *Where do you feel safest now?*

Now, reflect on how your definition of safety has evolved and what your Soul child still longs for.

Exercise: Building a Safe Space

- Go to a quiet area or any place you feel calm.
- Close your eyes and imagine creating a room or space just for your Soul Child.
- Fill it with objects, colors, or sounds that bring comfort.
- When you are ready, visualize inviting your Soul Child into that space and gently affirm: "You are safe here."

If it feels comfortable, use this page to sketch, doodle, or color your Soul Child's safe space. You don't have to be an artist, this is about expression, not perfection. Let symbols, shapes, or colors show what safety feels like for you.

Worksheet: My Safety Plan

Use the prompts below to design your personal safety plan:

- *A place where I feel safe is…*

- *A person who helps me feel supported is…*

- *An activity that calms me is…*

- *A phrase I can tell myself when I feel unsettled is…*

- *One way I can create safety in my daily life is…*

Music Reflection

Choose a song that makes you feel calm or reassured. As you listen, imagine playing it for your Soul child. How does it shift their emotions? How does it shift yours? Write down the feelings and images that come up as the music plays.

Closing Takeaway

By exploring what safety means to you, you've begun to lay the foundation your Soul Child has always needed. Safety is not just the absence of fear — it is the presence of comfort, compassion, and care. When you imagine a safe space, or when you create safety in your daily life, you are telling your Soul Child: "You belong here. You are protected. You are worthy of kindness."

Closing Reflection

Take a few moments to write what you want to carry with you from this chapter:
- A new understanding I have about safety is…
- One way I can practice compassion toward myself is…
- When I feel unsafe, I can remind myself…

(Use the space below to reflect or create your own safety reminders.)

_____

_____

_____

_____

_____

_____

_____

_____

_____

_____

Affirmation: "I create safety and compassion for my Soul Child. I am gentle, I am kind, and I am safe within myself."

GIVING VOICE TO YOUR SOUL CHILD

Why "voice" matters

As children, many of us learned that our feelings were "too much," our needs were inconvenient, or our truths were safer left unsaid. Over time, we adapted by getting quiet—hiding our disappointment, swallowing grief, tucking away anger, and even minimizing joy. That silence often protected us then. But as adults, it can muffle our confidence, our boundaries, and our capacity to connect.

Giving voice to your Soul Child is not about staying stuck in the past. It's about offering your younger self what they needed: presence, protection, and permission. When you listen without judgment and respond with compassion, you update an old story. You become the steady adult who says, "I hear you. You make sense. I'm here now."

How to Listen to Without Correcting)

When you open space for your Soul Child, it's natural to want to edit, explain, or soften what comes up. But this chapter invites a new kind of listening that values presence over perfection.

Whenever a memory or feeling surfaces, resist the urge to say, "That's silly" or "I should be over this by now." Instead, pause. Let it be. Your only job is to listen with compassion. Notice the words or memories you want to skip, hide, or dismiss because those are often the ones that most need to be heard. Name what feels true, not what feels reasonable. Your Soul Child speaks through emotion, not logic.

Write what feels real in the moment, even if it sounds messy, dramatic, or childish. Let every word belong. You don't need to fix, analyze, or solve — just witness. And if nothing comes to mind, that's perfectly okay too. Silence can be its own kind of healing.

Reflection: When Was Your Voice Silenced?

- Can you remember a time when you wanted to speak but were told to be quiet?
- What specific words or feelings did you hold inside?
- Where did you feel it in your body then (throat, chest, stomach)? Where do you feel it now?
- How did it feel to not be heard—alone, small, angry, confused?
- How might that experience still affect you today?
- What would it be like to let a small, safe version of your voice out now?

Exercise: Writing from the Voice of Your Soul Child

Use the next page to complete this exercise.

Setup

- *Take a deep breath and picture your younger self in a place they felt most safe or familiar.*

Write

- *Let your Soul Child speak in their own words. Don't edit or censor. Begin with prompts like:*
- *"I wish someone had told me…"*
- *"I felt…"*
- *"I needed…"*

Respond

- *When you finish, write a short response back as your adult self. Keep it simple and kind:*
- *"I hear you."*
- *"You were never too much."*
- *"I'm here now."*

Close

- *Thank your Soul Child: "Thank you for trusting me." Take one slow breath and return to the present.*

Exercise: Writing from the Voice of Your Soul Child

Worksheet: What My Soul Child Wants to Say

- *Something I always wanted to say but couldn't was…*
- *What I needed you to know was…*
- *I wish you had seen that I…*
- *Today, if I could shout it out loud, I'd say…*
- *The words I longed to hear were…*

_____

_____

_____

_____

_____

_____

Adult Self Response:
- *Today, I will…*
- *I promise to…*
- *You can count on me to…*

_____

_____

_____

_____

Music Reflection

Find a song that makes you feel seen or understood. Play it while imagining your Soul Child listening alongside you.

- *What do you notice in your body?*
- *Do they relax, cry, smile, or grow still?*
- *Write about the moment in detail. What lyric or sound felt like a hand on your shoulder*

_____

_____

_____

_____

Closing Reflection

- *What surprised you about what your Soul Child wrote?*
- *Which feelings were hardest to allow—and which felt like relief?*
- *What one boundary, ask, or kindness will you practice this week to honor their voice?*

_____

_____

_____

_____

Closing Takeaway

Your voice doesn't need to be loud to be true. Each time you allow your Soul Child to speak without judgment, you loosen the old knot of silence. This is how self-trust is rebuilt—one gentle listening at a time.

Affirmation: "I"My voice matters, and I listen with love."

REPARENTING YOUR SOUL CHILD

What It Means to Reparent Yourself

Many of us grew up with caregivers who did their best but could not always give us what we most needed—whether that was unconditional love, steady encouragement, patience, or safety. Sometimes they were distracted, overwhelmed, or carrying their own unhealed wounds. Often, parents were simply working with the tools and resources they had at the time. For some, poverty, lack of support, or daily stress left little energy for emotional nurturing. For others, their own unresolved trauma and pain made it difficult to be consistently present and attuned.

The result is that our Soul Child may have felt abandoned, unseen, or unsupported at critical moments. Those unmet needs do not disappear as we grow older. Instead, they often show up in adulthood through the ways we relate to ourselves and others— seeking constant validation, struggling to set boundaries, being overly critical, or feeling unworthy of love. These patterns are your Soul Child's way of saying, "I still need care."

Reparenting is the gentle, powerful practice of answering that need. It is not about blaming or rejecting the people who raised you. Rather, it is about recognizing that you, as an adult, can now step into the role of the supportive parent your younger self longed for. You can offer yourself comfort, structure, encouragement, patience, and protection—consistently and without condition.

Think of reparenting as building a home within yourself. It is a place where your Soul Child feels safe to rest, play, and grow. Each time you show up with patience and kindness, you create new patterns of stability and love. This is how you begin to feel rooted in self-trust and belonging.

Reflection: What Did You Need Most?

Take a moment to think back to your childhood. Close your eyes if it helps.
Then gently explore:

- *What is one thing you needed most but didn't consistently receive?*
- *Was it affection, encouragement, patience, or protection?*
- *How do you still seek that need today—in relationships, work, or the way you speak to yourself?*
- *How might you begin meeting that need for yourself now?*

Journal for 5 minutes. Be honest and simple. One word is enough if that's all that comes.

_____

_____

_____

_____

_____

_____

_____

_____

_____

_____

_____

_____

_____

_____

_____

_____

Worksheet: My Reparenting Plan

As a child, I longed for...

_____

_____

_____

Today, I can give myself...

_____

_____

_____

A phrase I wish I had heard is...

_____

_____

_____

i can begin practicing this by...

_____

_____

_____

i can begin practicing this by...

_____

_____

_____

Exercise: Becoming the Parent You Needed

Write down the qualities of a safe, loving parent.
(Examples: kind, patient, encouraging, protective)

_____

_____

_____

_____

For each quality, list one small way you can embody it for yourself today.
(Write your actions below, one per line).

_____

_____

_____

_____

Choose one to practice this week. (Circle, highlight, or write the quality you will focus on.)

This week, I will practice:

_____

_____

_____

_____

Music Reflection

Think of a song that feels nurturing or protective. Sing, hum, or play it as though you are singing it to your Soul Child.

- *What emotions rise up as you listen?*
- *What does your Soul Child seem to feel, relief, comfort, sadness, joy?*
- *Write a short reflection on what it feels like to step into this caregiver role.*

_____

_____

_____

_____

Closing Reflection

- *What surprised you about what your Soul Child wrote?*
- *Which feelings were hardest to allow, which felt like relief?*
- *What one boundary, ask, or kindness will you practice this week to honor their voice?*

_____

_____

_____

_____

Closing Takeaway

Your voice doesn't need to be loud to be true. Each time you allow your Soul Child to speak without judgment, you loosen the old knot of silence. This is how self-trust is rebuilt. One gentle listening at a time.

Affirmation: "My voice matters, and I listen with love."

BUILDING BOUNDARIES AND EMPOWERMENT

Healing the Space Between You and the World

Healthy boundaries are essential for protecting your Soul Child. They are the invisible lines that define where you end and where others begin. Boundaries are not punishments or walls; they are expressions of self-respect, clarity, and care. They tell the world, "This is how I can love you without losing myself."

For many of us, boundaries were not modeled or respected during childhood. Some were taught that having limits was wrong and that saying no meant being selfish, disrespectful, or ungrateful. Others were given no boundaries at all, left to navigate life without structure, protection, or permission to take up space. Still others experienced deep violations of their boundaries when their privacy, their belongings, or even their bodies were treated as if they did not belong to them.

If you grew up in an environment where your boundaries were ignored or never acknowledged, it is understandable if you now struggle to recognize what is acceptable and what is not. You may overgive to feel loved, stay silent to avoid conflict, or feel guilty for protecting yourself.

This chapter meets you wherever you are, whether you never learned what a boundary is or you are rebuilding the ones that were broken. Together, we will explore how boundaries are not barriers to love but pathways to healthy connection. They help your Soul Child feel safe, respected, and empowered enough to finally say:
"This is my space. This is my voice. This is my peace."

You deserve relationships that honor your "yes" and respect your "no." You deserve to feel in control of your body, your time, and your energy. Most importantly, your Soul Child deserves to know that it is safe to have needs and safe to protect them.

Reflection: Your Early Boundaries

Take a few moments to reflect on these questions:
- *Were you allowed to say no as a child?*
- *How did adults respond when you tried to set limits?*
- *Do you find it easy or difficult to set boundaries now?*

Take a moment to reflect on how your early experiences shaped your current boundaries. Do you tend to overextend yourself, or do you shut down and withdraw? Awareness is the first step toward change.

Exercise: Practicing Boundaries

1. Write down three situations in your life today where you struggle to set boundaries.
2. Next to each, write one sentence you could use to assert your needs respectfully.
3. Practice saying these sentences aloud to yourself in the mirror.
4. Notice how your body feels as you say them — empowered, nervous, shaky, strong? Write down your observations.

Worksheet: My Boundary Plan

As a child, I longed for…

_____

_____

_____

Today, I can give myself…

_____

_____

_____

A phrase I wish I had heard is…

_____

_____

_____

_____

_____

_____

I can begin practicing this by…

_____

_____

_____

Workbook Exercise: Reclaiming Your Boundaries

Think of three situations in your life today where you struggle to say no or where you feel drained. For each situation, write a boundary statement you could use to protect your energy. Example:

- "I can't take that on right now, but I appreciate you thinking of me."
- "That topic is uncomfortable for me, let's talk about something else."
- Practice saying these sentences out loud in front of a mirror.
- Notice your body's response — tension, lightness, resistance, relief. These sensations are messages from your Soul Child.
- Afterward, journal about what emotions surfaced. Did your Soul Child feel empowered, scared, or proud?

_____

_____

_____

_____

_____

_____

_____

_____

_____

_____

_____

_____

Exercise: My Boundary Plan

Fill in the following prompts:

A boundary I wish I had set as a child was…

_____

_____

A boundary I need in my life today is…

_____

_____

A phrase I can use to protect my boundary is…

_____

_____

One boundary I will practice setting this week is…

_____

_____

_____

One boundary I will practice setting this week is…

_____

_____

_____

Music Reflection

Choose a song that makes you feel powerful, grounded, or confident. Something that stirs your inner strength. Play it while imagining your Soul Child standing tall beside you. Feel their posture, their breath, their energy as they realize it's safe to take up space.

Write down how the music influences your body and emotions:
- *Do you feel more solid or rooted?*
- *Do you feel a sense of relief or release?*
- *How does your Soul Child respond to this strength?*

_____

_____

_____

Closing Reflection

Building boundaries isn't about pushing people away — it's about teaching the world how to treat you. Reflect on this:

"Every time I say no to what harms me, I'm saying yes to my healing."

How might your relationships and daily life shift if you began honoring your limits without apology?

Closing Takeaway

Boundaries are acts of love not rebellion. They are how you show your Soul Child that their peace matters, that their comfort is valid, and that their needs are worthy of protection.

Affirmation: "I honor my boundaries as sacred. I protect my peace, my energy, and my Soul Child with love and confidence."

NURTURING HEALTHY RELATIONS

Our relationships often mirror the lessons, patterns, and survival strategies we learned in childhood. The ways we connect, withdraw, or communicate today are often echoes of what our Soul Child experienced long ago. If love once felt conditional, you may still feel the need to earn it. If you were criticized or dismissed, you may now expect rejection before it happens. If affection was inconsistent or unavailable, you may crave closeness yet fear vulnerability.

This chapter invites you to explore how your early experiences shaped your current relationships, not to place blame, but to bring awareness and healing. By understanding the emotional blueprint your Soul Child carried forward, you can begin to rewrite it with compassion and intention.

Sometimes, our adult relationships become mirrors that reflect our unresolved wounds. We may find ourselves drawn to people who feel familiar, even when "familiar" isn't healthy. The goal of this work is not to erase your past but to understand it so deeply that it no longer quietly controls your choices. As you learn to nurture the connection with your Soul Child, you'll begin to attract and sustain relationships rooted in authenticity, not fear ones that grow from mutual understanding rather than old patterns of survival.

Healthy relationships are built on mutual respect, trust, communication, and emotional safety. These qualities do not come automatically; they grow when we learn to recognize our patterns and gently choose new ways of relating. This process begins within, by learning how to meet your own needs, soothe your own fears, and honor your boundaries.

Whether your Soul Child grew up with neglect, conflict, or chaos, you have the power now to model what safe and nurturing connection feels like. Each step you take toward emotional honesty and healthy boundaries sends a message to your Soul Child:

"You are worthy of love that doesn't hurt, doesn't take too much, and doesn't make you disappear."

Reflection: Relationship Patterns

Before you explore your current relationships, pause and look back. The first connections we experience with parents, caregivers, siblings, or teachers become our blueprint for love.

Take a few quiet moments to consider the following:

- *How did the adults in your childhood show love and affection?*
- *Were there consistent role models of trust and support?*
- *Did love ever feel earned, withdrawn, or unpredictable?*
- *How do you typically respond to conflict in relationships today*

Reflect on which patterns feel healthy and which may come from old wounds that are ready to be healed.

1. Write down three situations in your life today where you struggle to set boundaries.
2. Next to each, write one sentence you could use to assert your needs respectfully.
3. Practice saying these sentences aloud to yourself in the mirror.
4. Notice how your body feels as you say them — empowered, nervous, shaky, strong? Write down your observations.

Exercise: Mapping Relationship Patterns

Use the next page to explore the relationships that shape your life.

1. In the center, write "Me" — this represents you today.
2. Around your name, draw circles for your closest relationships (family, friends, partners, or others who impact you). Label each one.
3. Beside each circle, jot down how you usually feel in that relationship — safe, anxious, distant, supported, drained, etc.
4. Look for themes or patterns:
   - Are you often the caregiver, fixer, or peacemaker?
   - Do you avoid conflict or overextend yourself to keep peace?
   - Do you long for closeness but fear being hurt or rejected?
5. Choose one relationship. It can even be your relationship with yourself — where you'd like to practice a healthier boundary or behavior.
6. Write one small step you can take this week to nurture it with honesty and balance.

My Cypher: The Circle of Relationships

Inspired by the flow of connection and energy, My Cypher represents the movement of relationships that shape and sustain you, the people who share your rhythm, lessons, and love. Reflect on who pours into you, who drains you, and where balance can be restored. Each layer of your cypher holds a different level of closeness, influence, and energy. At the center is you — grounded, aware, and connected to your Soul Child.

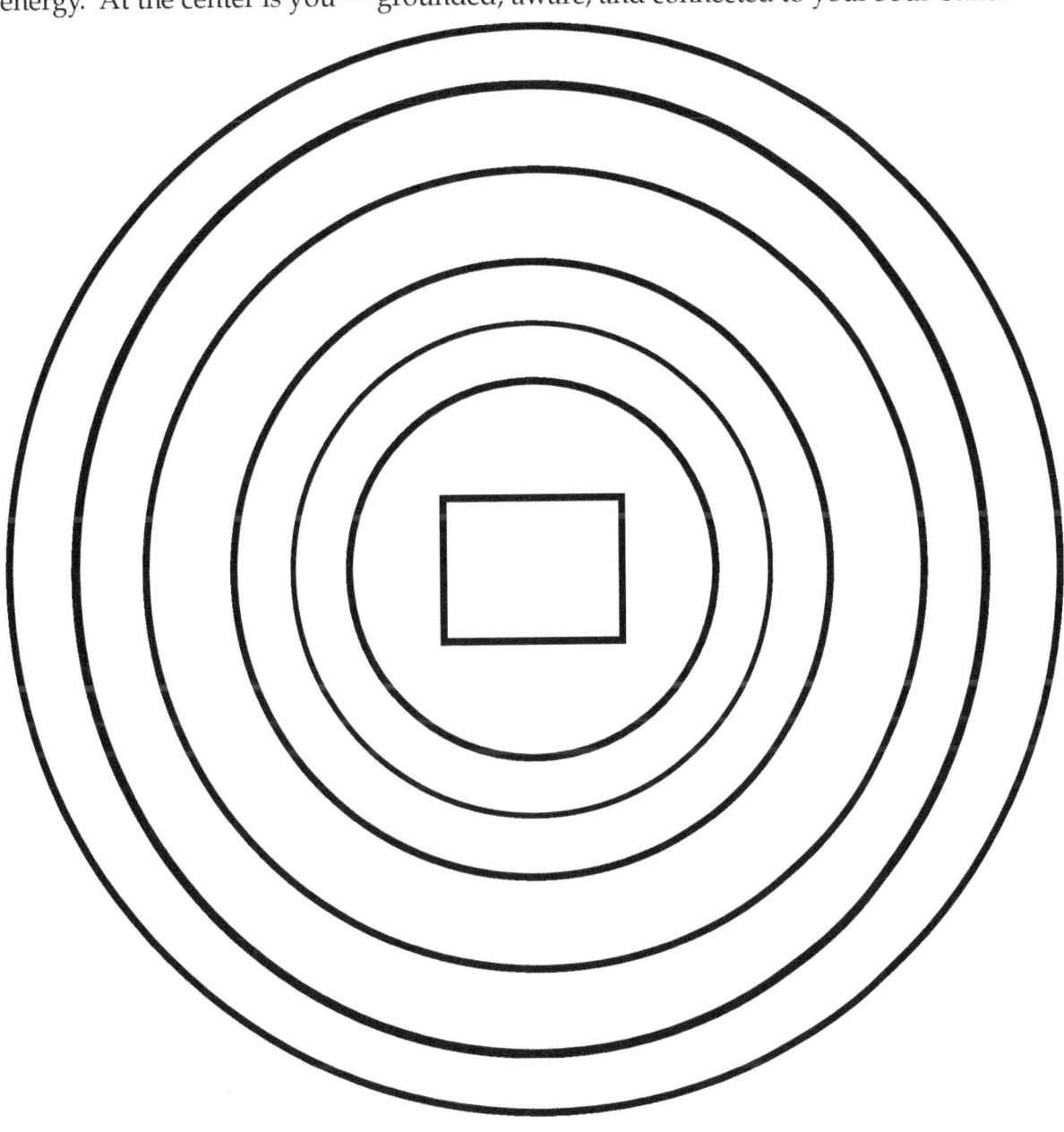

Exercise: Building Healthier Connections

Healthy relationships are not perfect — they are safe, balanced, and respectful. If you've never had that modeled for you, this exercise helps you envision what healthy connection could look and feel like.

My idea of a healthy relationship is...

_____

_____

A quality I want to strengthen in my relationships is...

_____

_____

One boundary that supports my peace and energy is...

_____

_____

When I honor my needs, I am teaching others that...

_____

_____

My Soul Child feels safe with people who...

_____

_____

Even if you've never had examples of healthy love, you can still learn to define it for yourself. This worksheet invites you to imagine — not what has been, but what is possible.

Music Reflection

Choose a song that reminds you of connection — friendship, love, family, or community. As you listen, imagine your Soul Child standing beside you, surrounded by people who see their worth and protect their joy. Let the lyrics or melody guide your heart toward what safe connection could sound and feel like. Afterward, write about the emotions or hopes that surfaced while listening.

_____

_____

_____

_____

Closing Reflection

Healthy relationships are not about perfection; they are about presence, safety, and truth. Every time you choose honesty over fear or clarity over avoidance, you teach your Soul Child that love can be kind, consistent, and mutual.
"I am learning what love feels like when it doesn't ask me to shrink."

Closing Takeaway

Healing your relationship patterns takes time, patience, and self-compassion. Each boundary you set, each need you express, and each moment of honesty you allow yourself is an act of reparenting your Soul Child. You are not too much. You are not unworthy. You are learning what it means to be loved in a way that honors who you truly are.

Affirmation: "I am open to love that feels safe, balanced, and kind. I attract relationships that honor my truth and nourish my Soul Child."

INTEGRATING YOUR SOUL CHILD INTO DAILY LIFE

Healing your Soul Child isn't a single breakthrough or a one-time act of reflection. It's a lifelong conversation between who you were and who you are becoming. Up to now, this workbook has helped you uncover your inner wounds, explore your needs, and begin to nurture that younger version of yourself with compassion. But awareness alone isn't enough; it must evolve into practice.

This chapter exists to help you build a bridge between insight and everyday living, between healing moments and your real, day-to-day choices. Integration is about allowing your Soul Child to exist beside you, not buried under layers of adulthood, obligation, or survival.

Many of us learned to keep our inner world quiet so we could function, appear strong, or survive environments that didn't feel safe. Over time, we became disconnected from joy, play, and rest, the very things that help the Soul Child thrive. This disconnection can show up in subtle ways: a constant rush, guilt for resting, or difficulty accepting love without fear.

Integrating your Soul Child into daily life is about rewriting that story. It's about transforming self-neglect into self-tending. When you make space each day, even briefly, to check in, to listen, or to nurture your inner world, you begin to live more whole and connected.

This chapter guides you through small, practical steps to make healing a habit rather than an event. The goal is not perfection; it's presence.

Reflection: Everyday Connection

- *How often do you pause to check in with your Soul Child?*
- *What daily activities already bring you comfort or spark joy?*
- *Where in your routine could you create more gentleness or self-compassion?*
- *How might daily awareness change the way you respond to stress or emotion?*

Reflect on how intentional awareness can become an act of re-parenting and stability.

The Daily Check-In

Each morning and evening, invite your Soul Child into your awareness.

1. *Begin by taking a few slow breaths. Imagine your younger self nearby.*
2. *Ask: "How are you feeling today?" Listen without judgment.*
3. *Write down a few words or sensations that come up.*
4. *Respond as the nurturing adult: "It's okay to rest," "I hear you," or "Let's find joy today."*
5. *Repeat this connection daily until it becomes a natural moment of mindfulness that keeps you emotionally aligned.*

Daily Practices

Use these prompts to create daily rituals that gently support integration:

- *A morning ritual that grounds and centers me is…*
- *A word or phrase I want to say to my Soul Child each day is…*
- *A playful or creative activity I will include weekly is…*
- *A way I can remind myself to slow down and listen is…*
- *At night, I can soothe my Soul Child by…*

Music Reflection: Daily Harmony

Music can become a bridge between your past and your present, a gentle way to stay connected with your Soul Child throughout daily life. Choose a song that feels like a daily anthem that lifts your mood, centers your spirit, or simply feels like "home" in sound form.

Play it during a morning ritual, while getting ready, or before bed. As you listen, notice how your body responds. Does your chest soften? Do your shoulders release? Does your Soul Child feel more seen or at peace?

After listening, reflect:
- *What emotion did this song awaken today?*
- *How can I carry this feeling into my day or evening?*
- *What does my Soul Child want me to remember when I hear this song?*

Use the same song daily for a week, or let your Soul Child choose a new one each morning, whatever feels right.

Closing Reflection

Healing isn't measured by how much pain you've processed but by how consistently you choose presence, care, and authenticity. Integration happens when your Soul Child begins to trust that they can show up, tired, joyful, anxious, or brave, and still be accepted.

Closing Takeaway

Integration transforms healing from an inward journey into an embodied way of living. Each mindful choice, a moment of rest, a kind word, a small joy, tells your Soul Child, "You belong in this life with me."

Affirmation: *"Each day, I honor my Soul Child by showing up with care and presence. I am learning to live with softness and strength — not apart from my past, but in harmony with it.*

LIVING AS A WHOLE, HEALED SELF

You've arrived at a turning point in your healing journey, a chapter that marks integration, not conclusion.

You've walked through memories, faced old pain with compassion, reclaimed your voice, and learned how to care for the child within you. Through reflection, music, and mindful practice, you've built a bridge between your past and present self.

This chapter is about wholeness, the quiet confidence that grows when you stop striving to be "fixed" and begin to live as your authentic self.

Healing isn't about erasing your history; it's about no longer letting the past dictate your present or define your worth. It's about offering your Soul Child a permanent home inside you, a place where they are safe, seen, and free to play, rest, and create.

At this stage, you may notice subtle but powerful changes: moments that once triggered fear or guilt now invite patience; you may pause instead of react, breathe instead of brace, forgive instead of replay. These shifts mean healing has taken root. The purpose of this chapter is to help you continue that integration, to live as the adult who honors and protects their Soul Child through daily choices and compassionate awareness.

Wholeness doesn't mean perfection. It means embracing every part of yourself, the light, the shadow, the tender, and the strong, and allowing them to coexist. It's granting yourself permission to feel joy again, to express freely, and to trust that you can live fully without abandoning the child within.

As you move through this chapter, know that your journey isn't ending; it's deepening. The next chapter will help you carry this wholeness forward, turning your healing practices into an ongoing rhythm, a lifelong relationship with your Soul Child.

Reflection: Signs of Integration

- *What moments recently made you realize you've grown?*
- *When do you feel most like your authentic self?*
- *What practices from this workbook do you want to carry forward?*
- *How can you remind yourself that healing is an ongoing relationship, not a final destination?*

Exercise: Wholeness in Action

- Reflect on one area of your life — work, relationships, self-care — where you feel more balanced now.
- Write down three small ways you can continue nurturing that growth.

_____

_____

- Identify one area that still feels tender or incomplete. What support, boundary, or routine could help you bring gentleness there?
- Write a short "promise to self" statement that unites your adult and Soul Child in shared care.

_____

_____

_____

_____

_____

_____

_____

Worksheet – Living as a Whole, Healed Self

One thing I have learned about my self while exploring my soul child...

_____

_____

A quality I want to strengthen in my relationships is...

_____

_____

I now understand that healing feels like...

_____

_____

When I notice myself slipping into old patterns, I will remind myself that...

_____

_____

A simple daily act that supports my wholeness is...

_____

_____

I will continue nurturing my soul child by...

_____

_____

_____

Music Reflection: Anthem of Wholeness

Find a song that feels like the soundtrack to your healing and mirrors where you are now, not where you've been. Play it while you close your eyes and imagine your Soul Child dancing beside you, laughing, unburdened.

Notice how the rhythm feels in your body. Let this song become your anthem of arrival — a melody that reminds you: you made it through.

After listening, write a few words about what "living whole" feels like for you today.

Closing Reflection

Wholeness is not the absence of pain — it's the presence of peace. It's knowing that your wounds no longer define you, your past no longer directs you, and your Soul Child is no longer waiting to be rescued. They have you now.

Closing Takeaway

Your healing is both a continuation and a homecoming. Every time you choose compassion, authenticity, or rest, you affirm the truth: you are already whole.

Affirmation: *"I live in harmony with all parts of myself. My Soul Child is safe, loved, and free within me. I move forward with softness, courage, and peace."*

Continuing the Journey

Healing doesn't end when the final page turns. It evolves.

By completing this workbook, you've reconnected with your Soul Child, faced painful memories with compassion, and learned how to nurture yourself with gentleness and truth. Now, the journey becomes about continuing — keeping your Soul Child close as you move through the changing seasons of life.

Integration is an ongoing dance. Some days you'll feel deeply connected and free; other days, old wounds may resurface. That's not failure — it's rhythm. Healing flows like music: sometimes soft and steady, sometimes full of emotion and movement. The key is to keep listening.

This chapter helps you create a long-term plan to maintain your healing practices — so your growth continues beyond these pages.

Reflection – Sustaining Growth

- How will you continue checking in with your Soul Child after this workbook ends?
- What practices from earlier chapters (journaling, boundaries, music, reflection) feel worth keeping in your weekly rhythm?
- What signs remind you that you're drifting away from your healing work — and how can you gently guide yourself back?
- Who or what supports your continued growth (friends, mentors, creative outlets, nature, spirituality)?

Creating Your Healing Maintenance Plan

- Choose three daily or weekly practices you can realistically maintain — such as journaling for five minutes, taking mindful walks, or listening to grounding music.
- Identify one monthly ritual — maybe revisiting a childhood hobby, writing a letter to your Soul Child, or reflecting on your emotional progress.
- Add one act of community: share your insights, connect with a support group, or create something that helps others heal.
- Keep this plan visible — in your journal, mirror, or phone — as a living reminder that healing isn't homework; it's devotion.

Worksheet – My Soul Child Healing Plan

One daily habit that keeps me grounded is…

_____

_____

A monthly check-in ritual I'll create is…

_____

_____

A person or space that supports my healing is…

_____

_____

When I feel disconnected, I can remind myself that…

_____

_____

A promise I make to my Soul Child today is…

_____

_____

I will continue nurturing my soul child by…

_____

_____

_____

Music Reflection: The Rhythm of Ongoing Healing

As you move forward, let music remain part of your healing ritual.
Choose a song that captures where you are now — a sound of calm, strength, or hope. Play it at least once a week as a way to reconnect. Let it become your "reset button."

Over time, create a Soul Child Playlist that represents healing, empowerment, love, and freedom.

Let each track be a reminder of how far you've come.

Closing Reflection

There is no finish line in healing — only expansion. You've created space within yourself for honesty, compassion, and joy. Carry these lessons with you as tools, not rules. Your Soul Child doesn't need perfection — only your presence.

Closing Takeaway

Healing is not a destination; it's a relationship that deepens with time. Keep showing up — softly, steadily, and sincerely.

Affirmation: *"My healing is ongoing, alive, and evolving. I walk forward whole, guided by love, truth, and the music of my Soul Child."*

BUT WAIT! THERE'S MORE!

A Companion Section for Ongoing Music Reflections & Journaling

If you grew up in the era of late-night infomercials, you might remember the familiar phrase: "But wait... there's more!" Just when you thought you'd seen it all, another surprise collection of timeless hits appeared, complete with an extra disc, a bonus song, or a heartfelt testimonial. This section is exactly that — your bonus collection—a place to continue your healing journey through rhythm, melody, and reflection.

You've done the deep work of self-awareness, boundaries, and reconnection. Now, these music-centered exercises invite you to play, to listen, and to feel again. Just like those "Greatest Hits" collections, this section gathers everything you've learned into something you can return to, whenever life feels loud, lonely, or a little offbeat. Think of it as your personal Soul Child Soundtrack: a lifelong playlist of healing, curiosity, and joy.

This section contains additional guided music reflections, affirmations, song suggestions, and blank pages for you to reflect. There's no right or wrong way to use these pages. You can move through them in order, skip around, or pick a reflection whenever your heart needs a tune-up. Use them alone during quiet moments, in therapy, or as a creative journaling tool. Healing is not linear, it's a symphony, and this is your encore.

Each reflection is music-based and designed for continued healing. You'll find guided prompts and journaling spaces to help you:
- Reconnect with memory through sound
- Explore emotion through rhythm
- Express healing through lyrical reflection
- Integrate music into daily self-care and mindfulness

All you need is your favorite playlist, a pen, and an open heart.

The Soundtrack of My Childhood

Goal: To access the emotional environment of your past through sensory memory.

- Create a playlist of 3–5 songs that played during or encapsulate the feeling of your childhood (e.g., a parent's favorite song, a genre that filled your home, or a lonely tune).

Journal Prompts:
- Listen to the playlist. What dominant emotion (fear, chaos, absence, love, or longing) does this soundtrack bring up?
- What age or age range does each song transport your Soul Child to?
- Speaking as your Adult Self, write a note of acknowledgment: "I see how this music shaped your world."
- Use the following page to write and reflect.

The Wounded Child's Mask

Goal: To identify the adult survival behaviors that stem from childhood pain.

- Choose a fast-paced, rhythmic song that mirrors your hustle, perfectionism, or people-pleasing energy.

Workbook Activity:
- List three major childhood needs that went unmet (e.g., safety, unconditional love, validation).
- Next to each need, identify the adult behavior (mask) you use to meet it now. Example → Unmet Need: Validation

_____   _____

_____   _____

_____   _____

A Name for the Pain

Goal: To personify and begin separating from the wounded Soul child's identity.

- Listen to a calm, instrumental piece that evokes feelings of patience and gentleness.

Journal Prompts:
- If your wounded Soul Child had another name (or a specific age), what would it be?
- What is the one thing this part of you most needs to say?
- In a few sentences, describe how you—the adult—can respond with compassion and protection.
- Use the following blank page to sketch, doodle, or jot a symbol that represents this part of you.

Emotional Resonance Check

Goal: To connect an emotion to its physical sensation.

- Play a short, intense piece of music (like a dramatic movie score) and note where tension lands.

Workbook Activity:
- Use the space below to draw a silhouette of a body.
- When you feel a trigger (anger, shame, fear), color in the area where you feel the sensation most strongly (e.g., anger in the fists, shame in the pit of the stomach).
- Identify the sensation (tightness, heat, tremor).

Trigger Breakdown

Goal: To trace a current emotional reaction back to its childhood root.

- Choose a song that makes you feel powerful and grounded—listen to it before and after the trigger analysis.

Journal Prompts:
- Recall a recent trigger.
- Follow this chain: Trigger Event → Emotion Felt → Immediate Thought → Childhood Memory/Belief (What did this event remind your Inner Child of?).
- You can use the song to recenter.
- Use the following page to write and reflect.

Reparenting the Critic's Script

Goal: To challenge the internalized negative messages from childhood.

- Listen to a lullaby or a gentle song you might play for a child.

Workbook Activity:
- Write down 3 phrases your inner critic constantly says to you (e.g., "You're not good enough"). "

_____

_____

_____

Write the Reparenting Response you would say to a child: "You are good enough, and I love you no matter what."

_____

_____

_____

_____

_____

_____

_____

_____

Lyrical Re-Visioning

Goal: To use songs to express emotions that are too hard to articulate directly.

- Choose a song with lyrics that perfectly describe your Soul Child's pain or trauma.

Journal Prompts:
- Write down the 5 most powerful lyrics.
- Write a new, alternative lyric for each of the 5 lines that reflects healing, safety, or hope.
- Read the new lyrics out loud, accompanied by the music.

The Unsent Letter

Goal: To safely release feelings of anger, abandonment, or unfairness towards caregivers or past situations..

- Play a piece of instrumental music that builds in intensity and then resolves (e.g., a crescendo followed by a calm resolution).

Workbook Activity:
- On a blank sheet of paper, preferably not from this workbook, write a letter to the person or situation that caused your Soul Child pain.
- Write until the emotion is fully on the page.
- **Do not send this letter.** The purpose is release. Destroy (rip, burn safely, or delete) the letter once complete.

The Primal Scream (Toned)

Goal: To physically release stored tension and emotion through sound.

- Select a song that has a long, sustained note or a steady, vibrational chord (like a drone or Tibetan singing bowls).

Body Work:
- With the music playing, focus on a difficult emotion.
- When the music reaches a suitable point, allow a toned sound (a deep hum, an audible sigh, or a controlled vocal tone) to escape, letting the vibration move through your body.
- Use the following page to journal afterwards.

Somatic Soundscape (Deep Dive)

Goal: To establish the feeling of safety in the body using sound and breath

- Use your pre-selected calming, instrumental music (432 Hz, nature sounds, slow piano).

Mindfulness Activity:
- Practice the anchor technique (hand on heart/belly) for 5-10 minutes.
- As you breathe with the music, imagine the sound waves filling your body, wrapping your Sould Child in warmth and protection.
- Focus on the feeling of being supported.

The Safe Place Duet

Goal: To create a vivid internal sanctuary that you can access instantly.

- Select a piece of ambient or nature-based music that feels perfectly secure and isolated from threat.

Guided Imagery:
1. Visualize your Soul Child in a "Safe Place" (real or imaginary).
2. Describe this place: the colors, the smells, what your Soul Child is doing.
3. Write a "Safety Mantra" based on the music's rhythm (e.g., "I am here, I am safe, I can breathe.").

Beat the Freeze Response

Goal: To interrupt the physical immobility that accompanies a "freeze" trauma response.

- Play a mid-tempo song with a strong, undeniable beat (one that makes you want to tap your foot).

Movement Practice:
If you feel overwhelmed or "frozen," put the song on.
Stand up and simply march in place, tap your feet, or gently sway.
Use the beat as a guide to bring small, controlled rhythmic movement back to your body.

The Empowerment Playlist

Goal: To internalize new, positive beliefs through lyrical and physical affirmation.

- Create a playlist of at least 5 songs with intentional, positive lyrics that you want to believe about yourself now.

Workbook Activity:
- For each song, identify the old, limiting belief (e.g., I am unlovable).
- Write the new, empowering belief.
- Play the song and do a power pose or dance while repeating the new belief, feeling the change in your body.

Revisioning the Memory

Goal: To provide the care and protection your Inner Child needed during a painful memory.

- Choose a song that evokes a feeling of strong, protective love (like a maternal/paternal embrace).

Visualization & Letter:
- Recall a specific hurtful memory.
- Visualize your Adult Self entering the memory. What do you say to the Soul Child version of you? What do you do to protect them?
- Use the next page or a separate sheet a paper to write a letter to your Soul Child starting: "I am here now. You are safe with me."

The Bridge to the Future

Goal: To integrate your healed Soul Child into your adult goals and decision-making

- Listen to a piece of inspirational music that sounds like a journey or an adventure.

Journal Prompts:
- What does your healed Soul Child want you to do for joy this week?
- How will you consult your Soul Child (for intuition and joy) before making a major decision?
- Write a promise to continue being the loving parent this child always deserved.

A Song of Commitment

Goal: To create a final, personal anthem for self-compassion. To establish the feeling of safety in the body using sound and breath

- Select one song to be your lifetime self-care theme song.

Final Pledge:
- Write a pledge to yourself about how you will show up for your Inner Child every day.
- Include at least three specific, small actions (e.g., "I will take five slow breaths when triggered," "I will dedicate 10 minutes to art," "I will honor my boundary").

_____

_____

_____

_____

_____

_____

_____

_____

_____

_____

The Gratitude Cadence

Goal: To shift focus from what was missing to what is present and possible.

- Play a song that makes you feel light, grateful, or joyful.

Workbook Activity:
- List 10 things your Adult Self has gained because of the Soul Child's resilience (e.g., empathy, strength, a desire for peace).
- Write 3 things you are grateful for today that would make your childhood self smile.

_____

_____

_____

_____

_____

_____

_____

_____

_____

_____

_____

The Soul Child Reprise

Goal: To reflect on your growth and create a lasting emotional connection through music.

Revisit Your Playlist

Go back through the songs you've collected or discovered while completing this workbook. Listen to a few of them in order, from your earliest memories to the songs that represent your healing. Notice how your emotional tone shifts as you move through time.

Choose Your Anthem

Select one song that feels like a reflection of your growth—not because everything is healed, but because you can feel movement within yourself. Let it be a song that speaks to who you're becoming: one that carries notes of freedom, peace, release, or renewal. As you listen, allow the lyrics, rhythm, or melody to fill the space around you. Notice where it lands in your body, what memories stir, and what parts of you begin to soften or rise.

Reflect and Write

After listening, journal your reflections:
- How does this song represent who you've become?
- What emotions or images rise up as you listen?
- What message would your Soul Child want to send me in this moment?
- What words of gratitude or commitment do you want to give back?

Let your writing flow freely. There's no right or wrong way to respond.

Closing Gratitude: The Music Continues

If you've reached this page, take a deep breath—you've done something extraordinary. You didn't just complete a workbook. You chose to meet yourself, listen to your Soul Child, and begin a process that many postpone for years.

The "Wait, There's More" section was a collection of extended reflections and music-based practices meant for those who wanted to go a little deeper. You didn't have to do them, but you did. That willingness to keep going, to explore the spaces beyond the assigned pages, speaks volumes about your commitment to your healing.

This moment is worth pausing for. Feel the weight of what you've uncovered, the truths you've written, and the strength it took to stay present with your story. Healing isn't linear, and it's never really finished. It's a lifelong melody — one that shifts, expands, and deepens with every choice to return to yourself. Some days it will sound like joy, others like rest. But it will always be yours.

Closing Reflection
- What part of this journey surprised you most?
- What moments brought you peace or clarity?
- How will you continue to nurture your Soul Child moving forward?

Takeaway Thought
Healing is not the absence of pain — it's the presence of compassion.

Affirmation: "I honor the courage it took to return to myself. My Soul Child and I walk forward together — whole, loved, and free."

Notes to The Soul Child

"Dear Soul Child,
If only you knew how brave you've been all along…"

Use the next few pages to write freely, doodle, or take notes. Some reflections might include letters to the younger version of yourself
 What do you want them to know today?
 What do you wish someone had told you?

Gratitude & Affirmations Page

Gratitude turns what we have into enough.
 Write short notes, phrases, or affirmations that make your Soul Child feel safe,
seen, and celebrated.
Prompts to get you started:

- "Today, I'm grateful for…"
- "A part of me that deserves more compassion is…"
- "I am learning to…"
- "My Soul Child reminds me that…"

Soul Child Recommended Songs

All song titles and artist names are referenced for reflective and educational purposes only.

Full rights remain with their respective copyright owners.

This workbook does not reproduce or distribute any lyrics or music and is not affiliated with the listed artists or publishers.

1. NEO SOUL & R&B (Validation and Self-Commitment)

Artist	Song Title	Genre & Vibe	Inner Child Vibe / Reparenting Vibe	Suggested Use in Workbook
India.Arie	"Get It Together"	Neo Soul/R&B - Confrontation & Ownership	**Inner Child/Reparenting:** Directly addresses the pain caused by "kin" and challenges the listener to take responsibility for their own healing. A crucial shift from pain to power.	**The Unsent Letter (Ch. 3):** Use as a guiding track before writing to a family member who caused pain, or before the vow to forgive.
Aliah Sheffield	"Some of Your People"	Alternative R&B/Vocal - Introspection & Truth	**Inner Child:** Addresses the difficult, often taboo truth that your closest "people" can inflict the deepest wounds. Validates feelings of betrayal and isolation.	**A Name for the Pain (Ch. 1):** Essential for the section on acknowledging the *source* of the wound without minimizing the severity.
Beyoncé	"I Care"	R&B/Soul Ballad - Self-Validation	**Inner Child/Reparenting:** Acknowledging the pain of not being seen, followed by the empowering realization of self-care.	**A Name for the Pain (Ch. 1):** Use while processing the neglect felt by the inner child.
Jill Scott	"Golden"	Neo Soul - Freedom & Self-Worth	**Reparenting:** The ultimate anthem of self-acceptance and living authentically.	**The Empowerment Playlist (Ch. 5):** Core song for affirming the new, authentic self.
Beyoncé	"Me, Myself and I"	R&B/Pop - Self-Reliance	**Reparenting:** The anthem of committing to yourself first.	**The Safe Place Duet (Ch. 4):** A core song for making the self-commitment vow.

The "Soul Child" Healing Playlist suggestions

2. GOSPEL & CONTEMPORARY R&B (Hope and Presence)

Artist	Song Title	Genre & Vibe	Inner Child Vibe / Reparenting Vibe	Suggested Use in Workbook
Kirk Franklin	"Everything Will Be Alright"	**Gospel/Soul - Divine Reassurance**	**Reparenting:** Focuses on the core belief that you are never too far gone to return to self/source and that hope is constant.	**The Empowerment Playlist (Ch. 5):** Use for deep moments of anxiety, reinforcing radical acceptance and hope.
PJ Morton	"Better"	**Gospel/R&B - Hope & Perseverance**	**Reparenting:** An uplifting track that focuses on the promise of improvement and internal support.	**The Empowerment Playlist (Ch. 5):** Use for motivating action and reinforcing a positive future.
Infinite Coles	"Dad and I"	**Alternative/Indie R&B - Introspection & Yearning**	**Inner Child:** Addresses complex parental relationships, the search for authentic connection, and inherited trauma.	**The Unsent Letter (Ch. 3):** Highly effective for processing complex feelings toward a parent or parental figure.

3. COUNTRY ROCK & AMERICANA (Resilience and Moving On)

Artist	Song Title	Genre & Vibe	Inner Child Vibe / Reparenting Vibe	Suggested Use in Workbook
Chris Stapleton	"Starting Over"	**Country Soul/Rock - Rebirth & New Beginnings**	**Reparenting:** A powerful song about leaving the past behind, finding comfort in the unknown, and focusing on the path ahead.	**The Safe Place Duet (Ch. 4):** The official "New Journey" song, celebrating the first steps of the healed life.
Jason Isbell and the 400 Unit	"Anxiety"	**Americana/Southern Rock - Acknowledgment & Honesty**	**Inner Child:** Directly addresses the struggle with anxiety, giving voice to the frustrated inner child overwhelmed by fear.	**A Name for the Pain (Ch. 1):** Use to validate the feeling of being trapped by mental health struggles.

Author's Closing Note

Dear Reader,

You've done something remarkable. By opening these pages and daring to look within, you've taken the first courageous steps toward healing your Soul Child. This work isn't easy — it asks for honesty, tenderness, and persistence. But every reflection, every boundary you set, every moment of self-kindness is an act of liberation.

Healing isn't about rushing to "fix" yourself. It's about returning home to the person you were before the world told you who you had to be. Your Soul Child has always been waiting for you — patient, hopeful, and ready to play again. As you continue this journey, remember: growth is not linear, and you are never behind. Some days you'll soar, and others you'll simply breathe — both are progress. Keep showing up. Keep listening. Keep singing your truth.

With love and belief in your healing,

Danita L. Ealy, MS, LPA, BCBA
Founder, Wallace Ealy Publishing

Resources for Ongoing Healing

If at any point during your healing journey you feel overwhelmed or need additional support, please reach out. You do not have to do this alone.

- 988 Suicide and Crisis Lifeline: Call or text 988 (24/7, confidential support)
- SAMHSA Helpline: 1-800-662-HELP (4357) for mental health and substance use services
- National Domestic Violence Hotline: 1-800-799-SAFE (7233) or text "START" to 88788
- Crisis Text Line: Text HOME to 741741
- Psychology Today's Therapist Directory — www.psychologytoday.com
- TherapyDen — www.therapyden.com
- Inclusive Therapists — www.inclusivetherapists.com
- Healing the Inner Child - https://nacoa.org/healing-the-inner-child-how-adults-can-support-their-younger-selves